HAL LEONARD
STUDENT
PIANO
LIBRARY

More Christmas Piano Solos

For All Piano Methods

Table of Contents

Book: ISBN 978-1-4234-8363-2
Book/CD: ISBN 978-1-4234-9328-0

HAL•LEONARD®
CORPORATION

7777 W. BLUEMOUND RD. P.O. BOX 13819 MILWAUKEE, WI 53213

Visit Hal Leonard Online at
www.halleonard.com

Angels from the Realms of Glory

Words by James Montgomery
Music by Henry T. Smart
Arranged by Jennifer Linn

Joyfully (♩ = 108)  TRACKS 1/2

Play both hands one octave higher throughout.

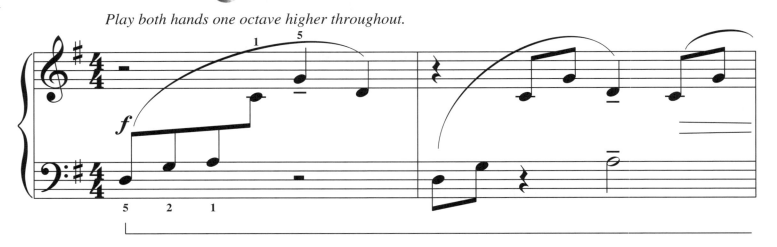

An - gels from the realms of glo - ry,
Sa - ges, leave your con - tem - pla - tions,

mp a tempo

wing your flight o'er all the earth.
bright - er vi - sions gleam a - far.

Ye who sang cre -
Seek the great de -

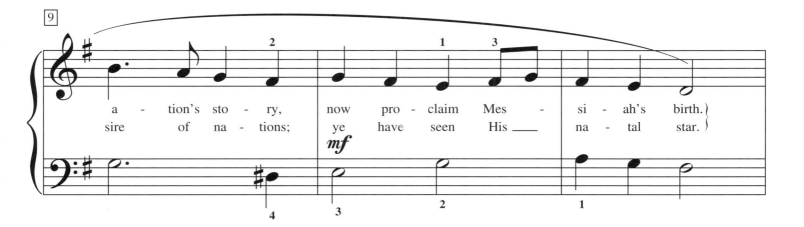

a - tion's sto - ry, now pro - claim Mes - si - ah's birth.
sire of na - tions; ye have seen His na - tal star.

mf

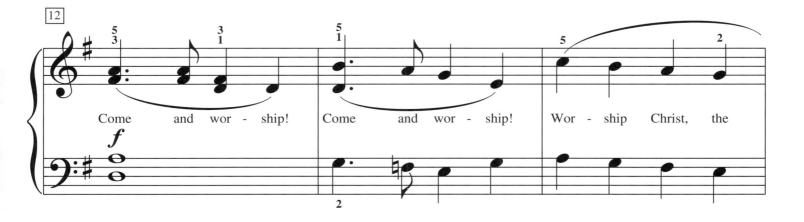

Come and wor - ship! Come and wor - ship! Wor - ship Christ, the

f

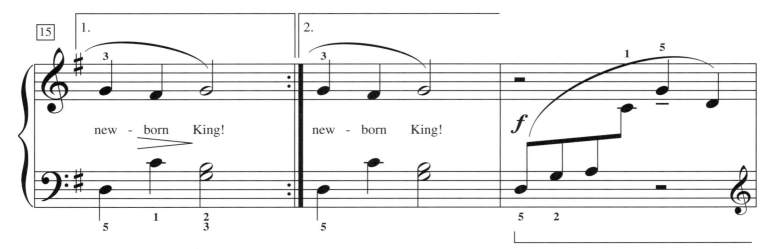

1.
new - born King!

2.
new - born King!

f

rit.

p

White Christmas

from the Motion Picture Irving Berlin's HOLIDAY INN

Words and Music by Irving Berlin
Arranged by Mona Rejino

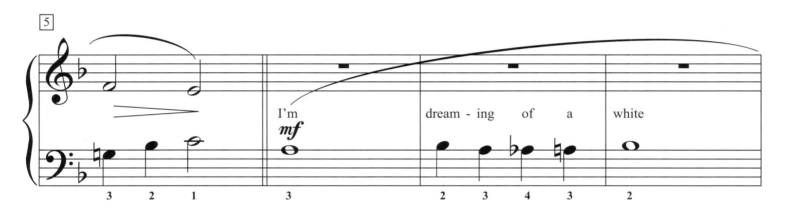

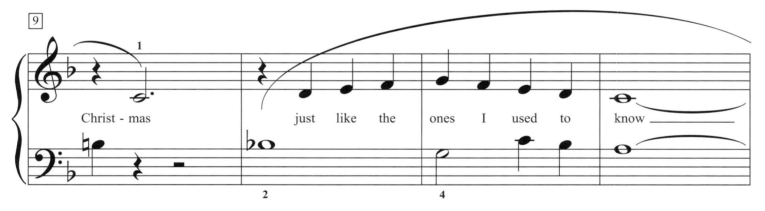

Accompaniment (Student plays one octave higher than written.) TRACKS 3/4

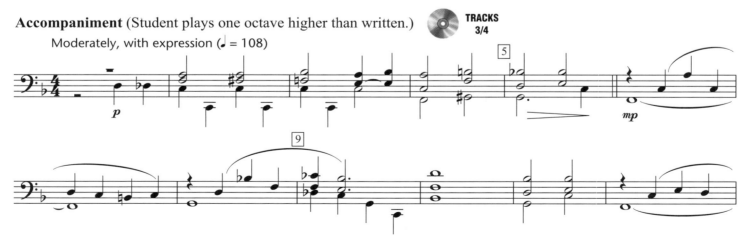

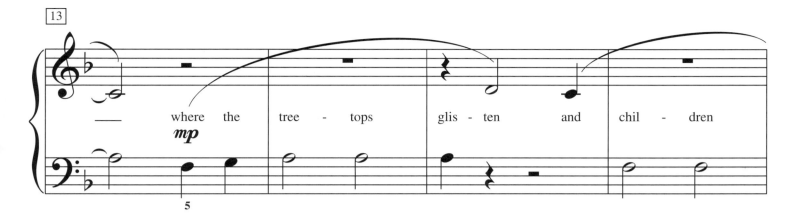

where the tree - tops glis - ten and chil - dren

mp

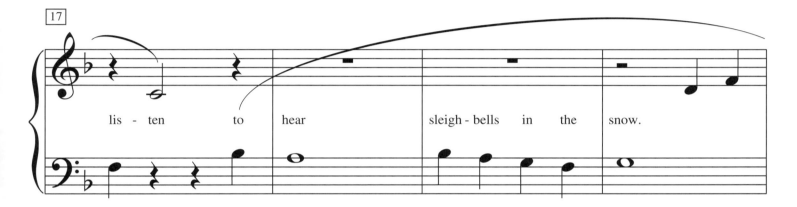

lis - ten to hear sleigh - bells in the snow.

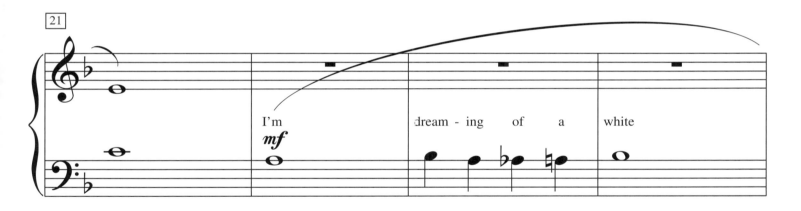

I'm dream - ing of a white

mf

p

mp

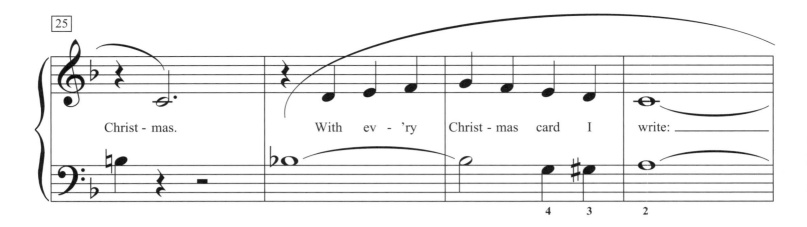

Christ - mas.   With ev - 'ry Christ - mas card I write: _____

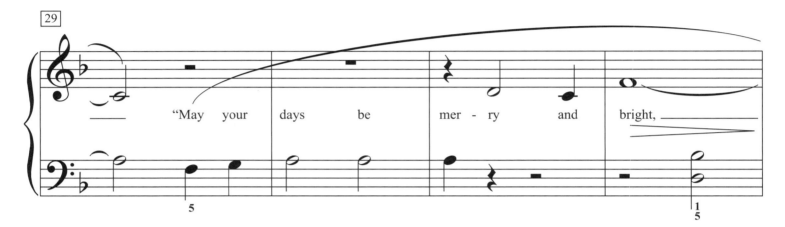

_____ "May your days be mer - ry and bright, _____

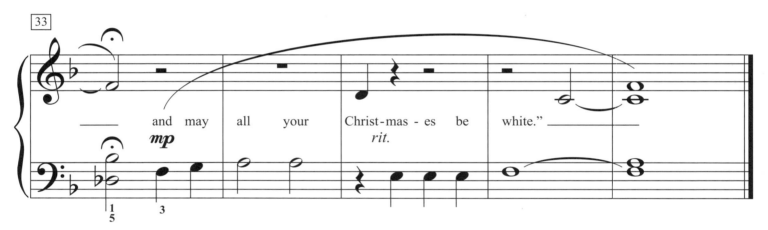

_____ and may all your Christ-mas - es be white." _____

mp   *rit.*

p   *rit.*

Christmas Time Is Here

from A CHARLIE BROWN CHRISTMAS

Words by Lee Mendelson
Music by Vince Guaraldi
Arranged by Phillip Keveren

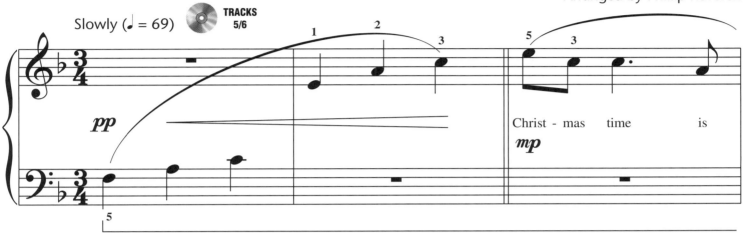

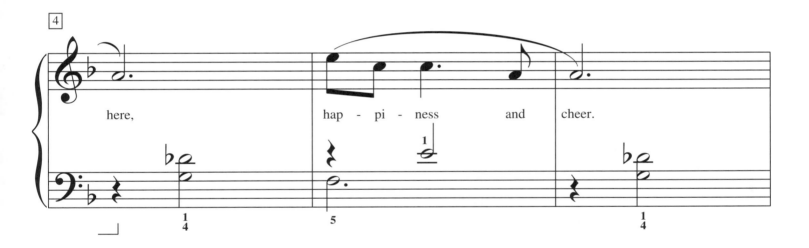

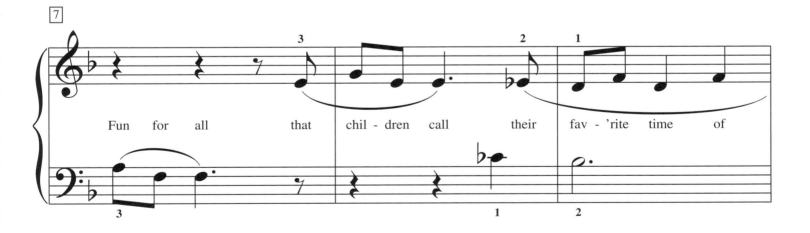

year. Snow - flakes in the air,

car - ols ev - 'ry - where. Old - en times and

an - cient rhymes of love and dreams to share.

Sleigh - bells in the air, beau - ty ev - 'ry -

mf *p*

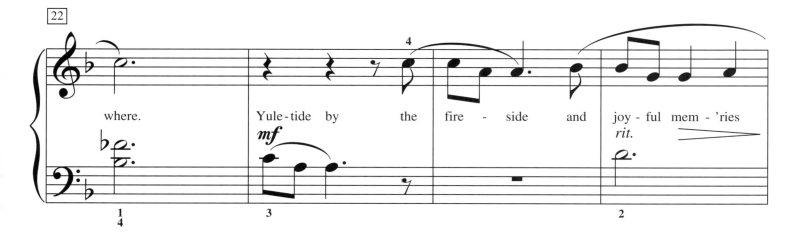

where. Yule-tide by the fire - side and joy-ful mem - 'ries

there. Christ-mas time is here, we'll be draw - ing

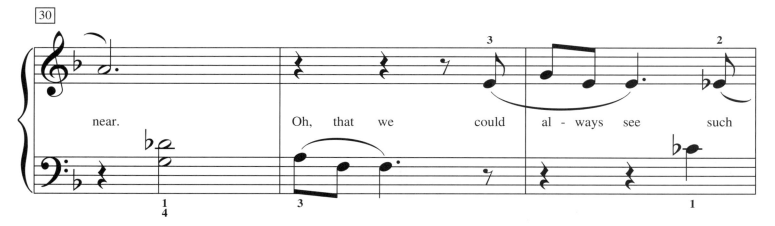

near. Oh, that we could al - ways see such

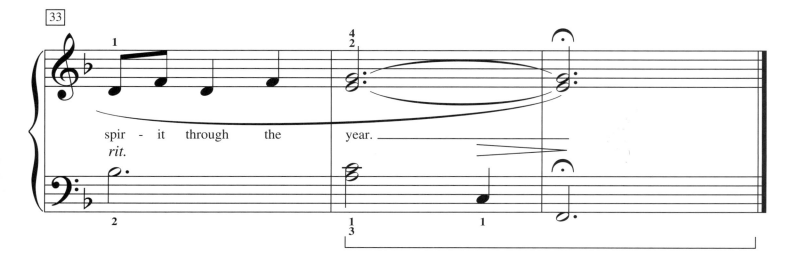

spir - it through the year.

Jingle Bells

Words and Music by
J. Pierpont
Arranged by Carol Klose

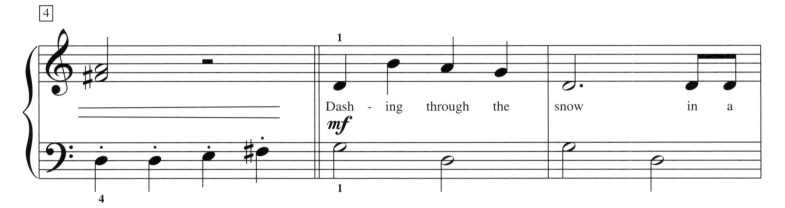

Dash - ing through the snow in a one - horse o - pen sleigh,

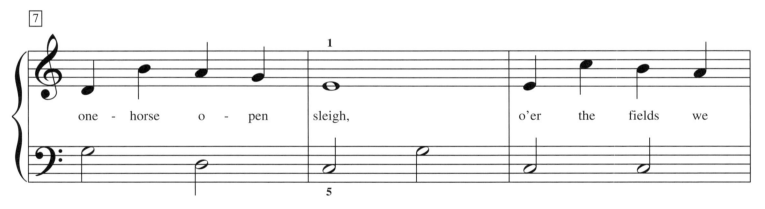

o'er the fields we

Accompaniment (Student plays one octave higher than written.) **TRACKS 7/8**

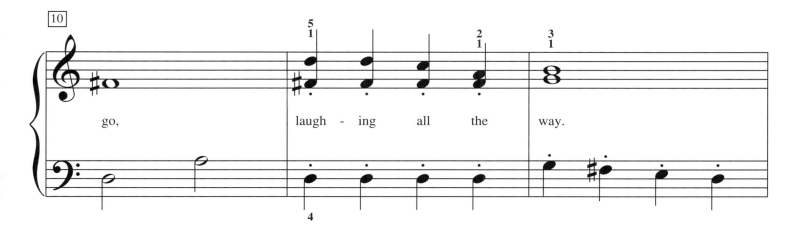

go,   laugh - ing   all   the   way.

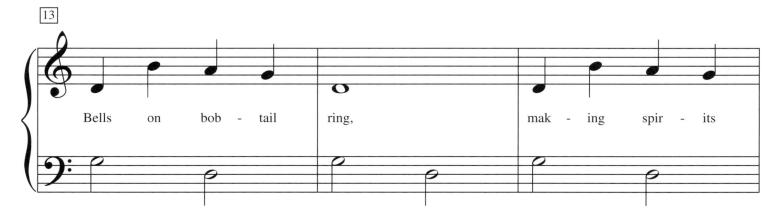

Bells   on   bob - tail   ring,   mak - ing   spir - its

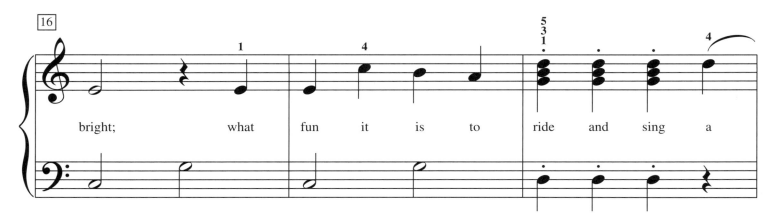

bright;   what   fun   it   is   to   ride   and   sing   a

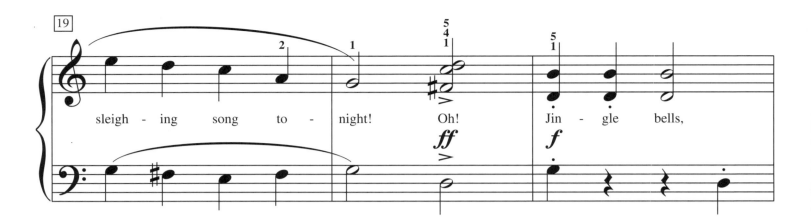

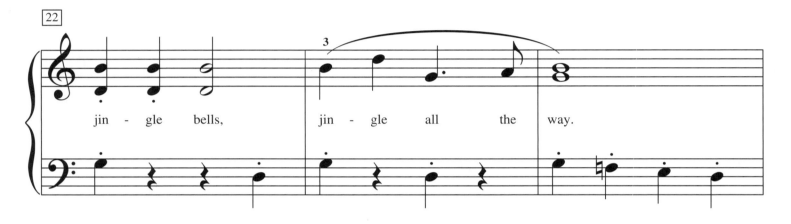

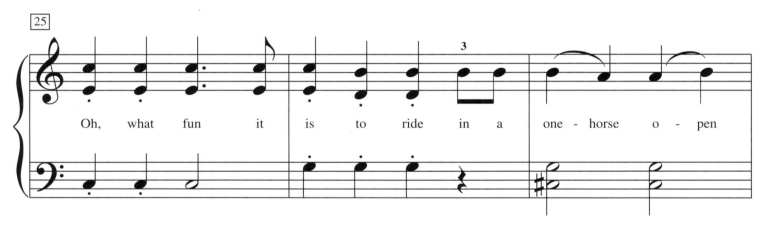

sleigh! Hey! Jin - gle bells, jin - gle bells,

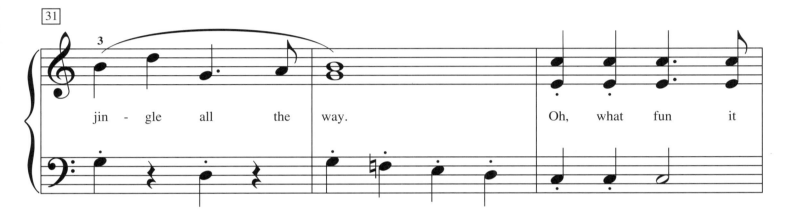

jin - gle all the way. Oh, what fun it

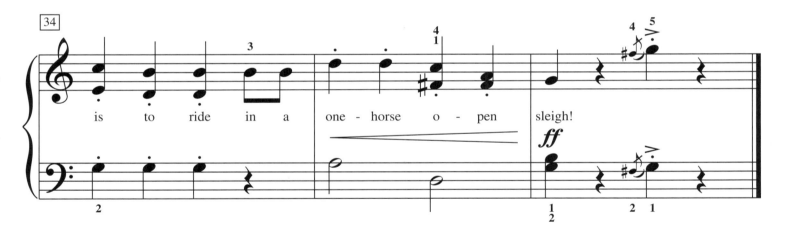

is to ride in a one - horse o - pen sleigh!

Once in Royal David's City

Words by Cecil F. Alexander
Music by Henry J. Gauntlett
Arranged by Phillip Keveren

With fanfare (♩ = 96)   TRACKS 9/10

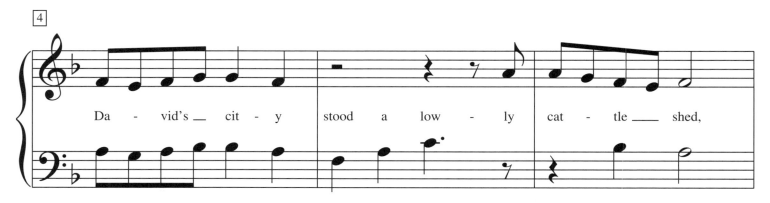

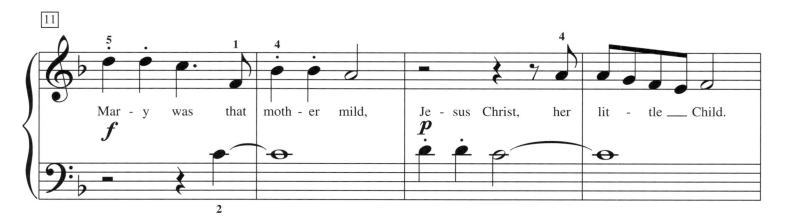

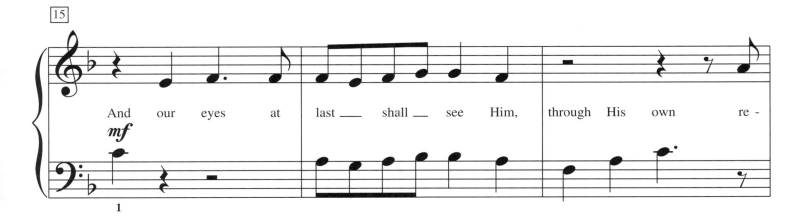

And our eyes at last ___ shall ___ see Him, through His own re-

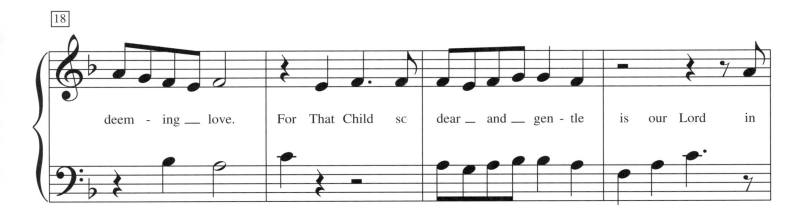

deem - ing ___ love. For That Child so dear ___ and ___ gen - tle is our Lord in

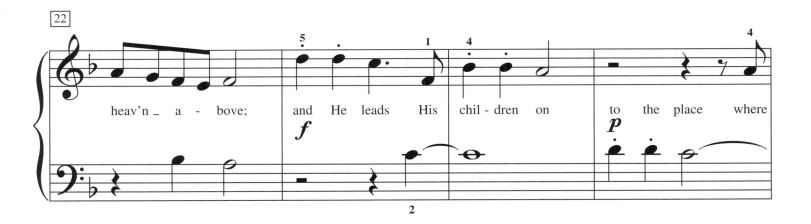

heav'n _ a - bove; and He leads His chil - dren on to the place where

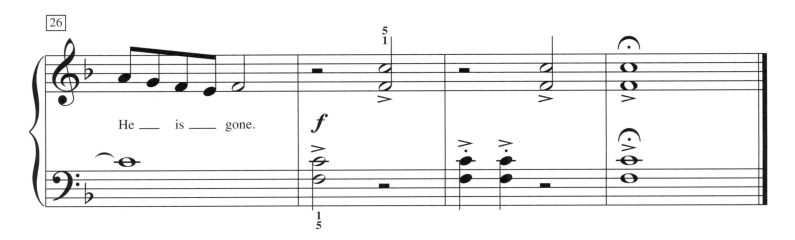

He ___ is ___ gone.

Here We Come A-Wassailing

Traditional
Arranged by Fred Kern

joy   come   to   you,   and   to   you   your   was - sail

too;   And   God   bless   you   and   send ____ you   a

mf

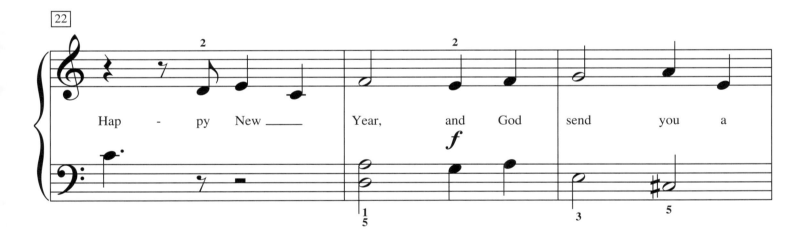

Hap - py   New ____   Year,   and   God   send   you   a

f

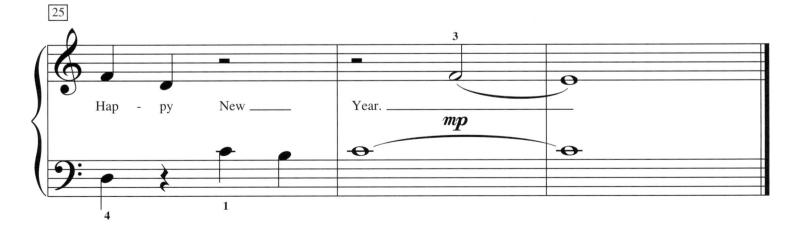

Hap - py   New ____   Year. ____

mp

Suzy Snowflake

Words and Music by Sid Tepper
and Roy Bennett
Arranged by Fred Kern

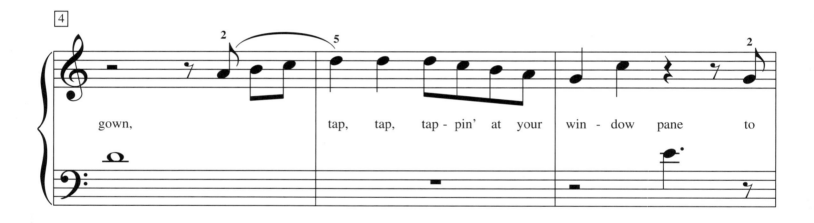

Here   comes   Su - zy   Snow - flake,   dressed in a   snow   white

gown,   tap,   tap,   tap - pin' at your   win - dow   pane   to

Accompaniment (Student plays one octave higher than written.)   **TRACKS 13/14**

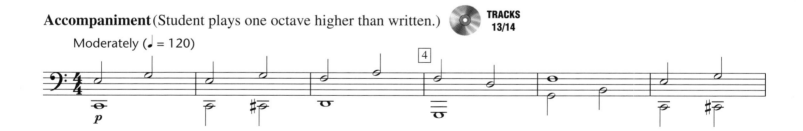

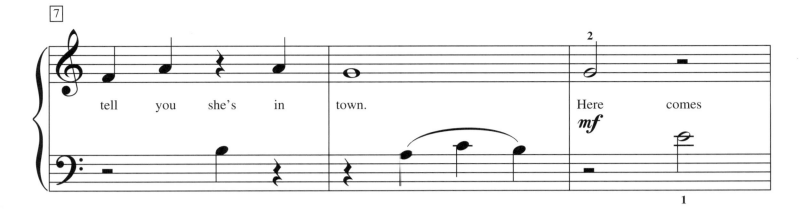

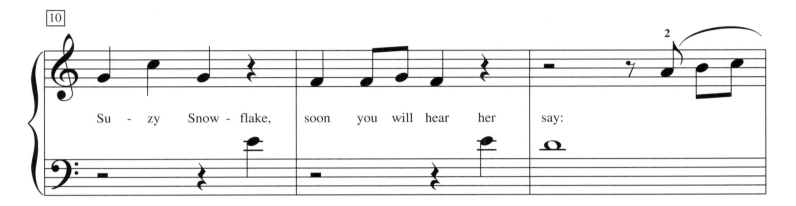

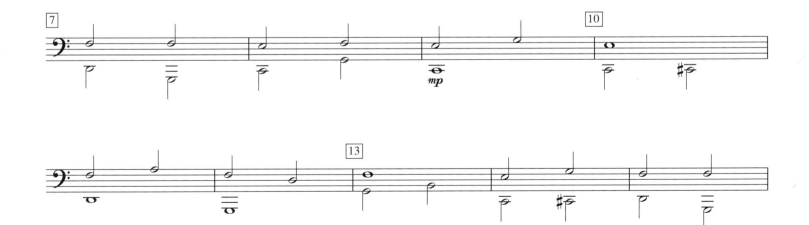

stay."   If you wan - na make a   snow - man

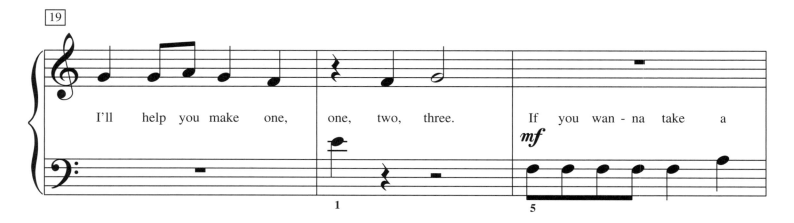

I'll help you make one,   one, two, three.   If you wan - na take a

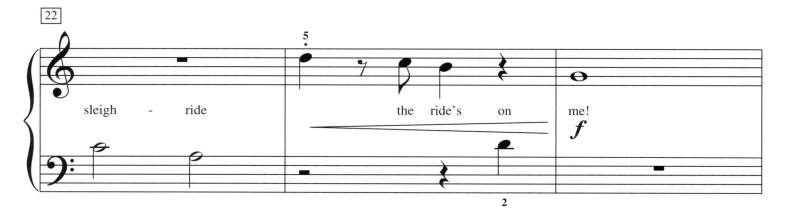

sleigh - ride   the ride's on   me!

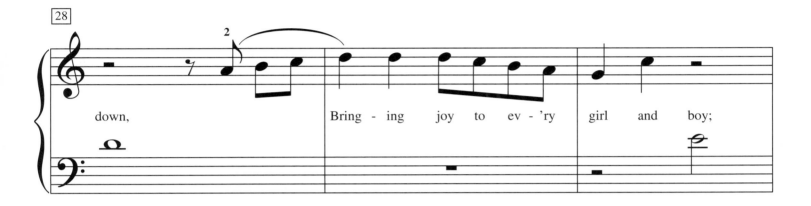

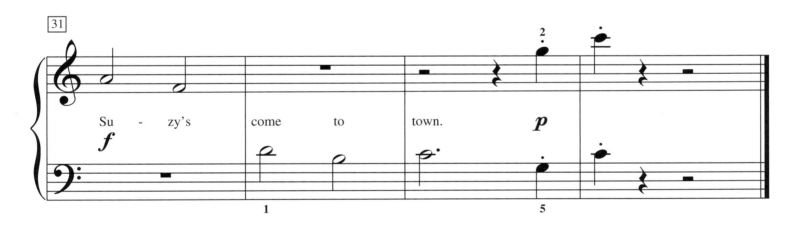

Blue Christmas

Words and Music by Billy Hayes
and Jay Johnson
Arranged by Phillip Keveren

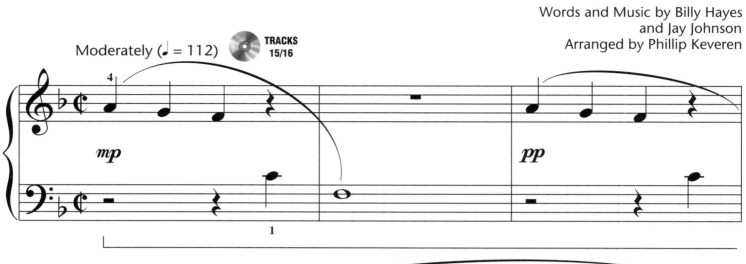

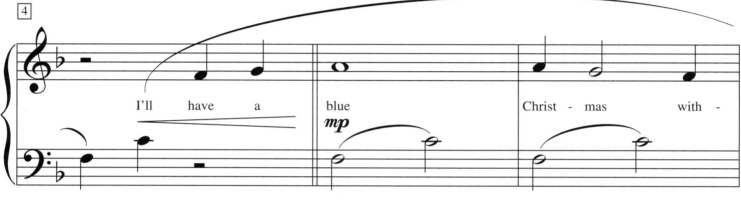

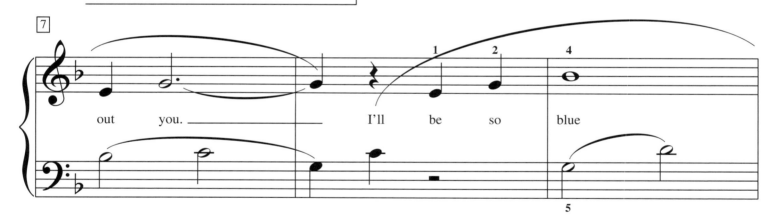

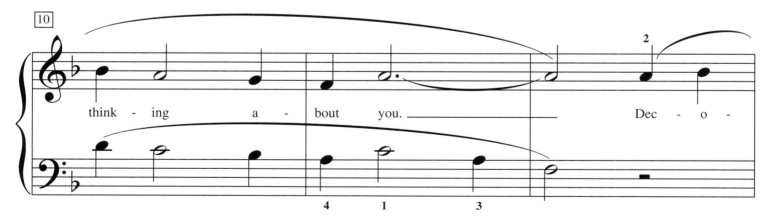

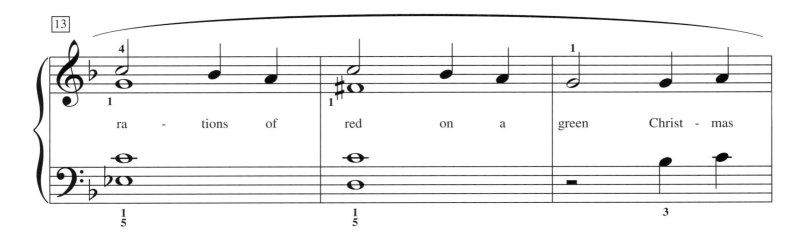

ra - tions   of   red   on   a   green   Christ - mas

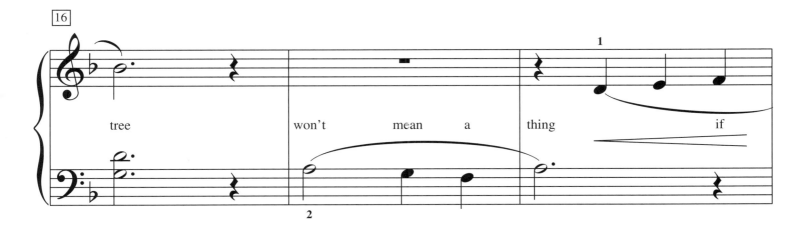

tree   won't   mean   a   thing   if

you're   not   here   with   me.   I'll   have   a   blue

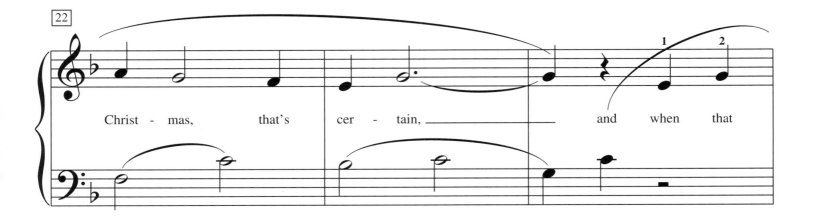

Christ - mas,   that's   cer - tain,_____   and   when   that

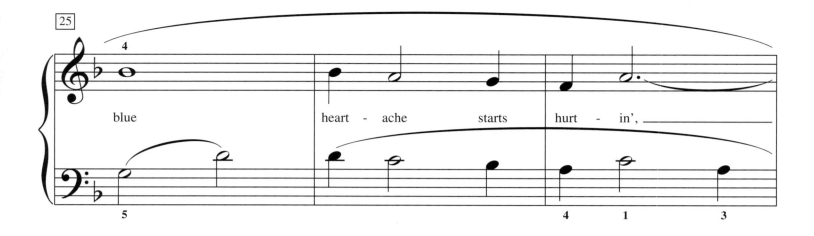

blue   heart - ache   starts   hurt - in', _____

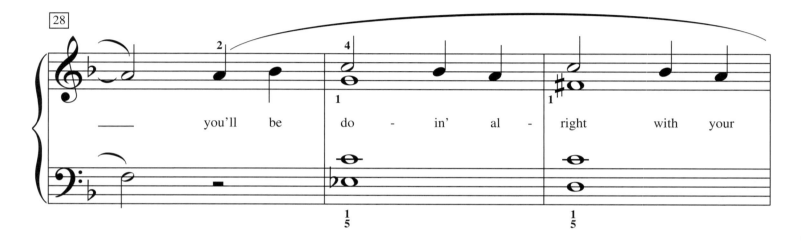

_____   you'll   be   do - in' al - right   with   your

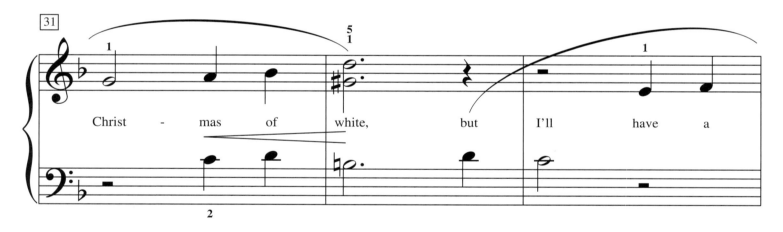

Christ - mas   of   white,   but   I'll   have   a

blue,   blue   Christ - mas.

I Saw Mommy Kissing Santa Claus

Words and Music by
Tommie Connor
Arranged by Mona Rejino

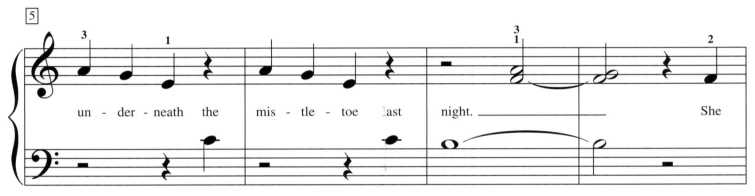

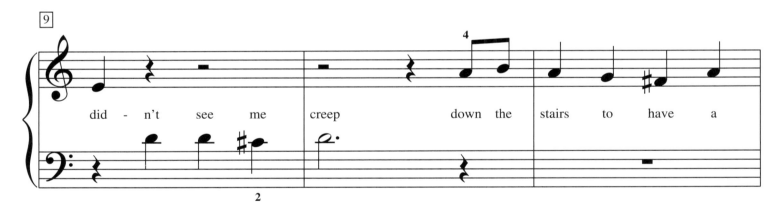

Accompaniment (Student plays one octave higher than written.) 🔘 **TRACKS 17/18**

peep; she thought that I was tucked up in my

bed - room fast a - sleep. Then I saw

Mom - my tick - le San - ta Claus, un - der - neath his

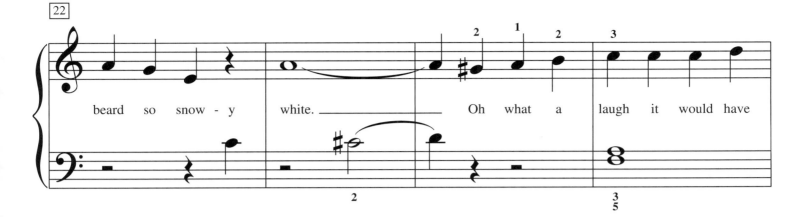

beard so snow - y white. _____ Oh what a laugh it would have

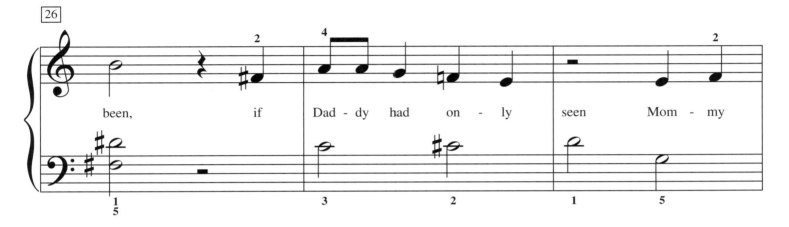

been, if Dad - dy had on - ly seen Mom - my

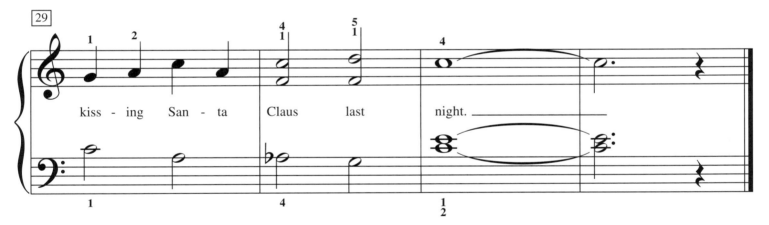

kiss - ing San - ta Claus last night. _____

Coventry Carol

Words by Robert Croo
Traditional English Melody
Arranged by Mona Rejino

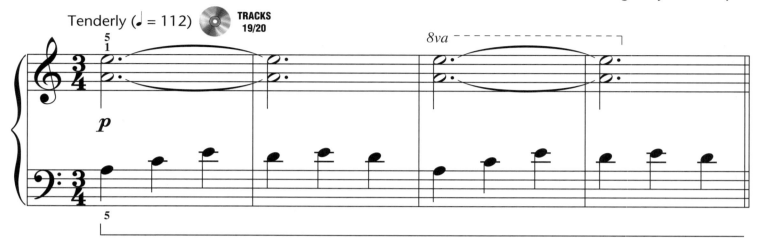

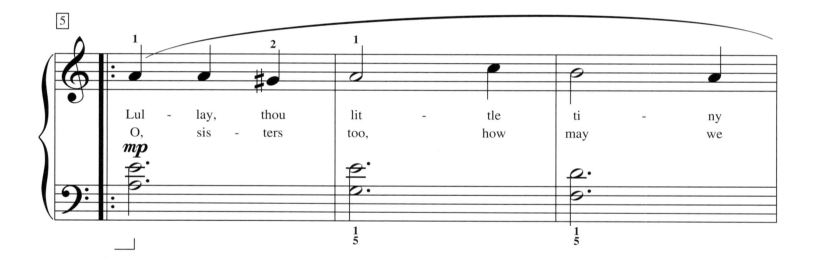

Lul - lay, thou lit - tle ti - ny
O, sis - ters too, how may we

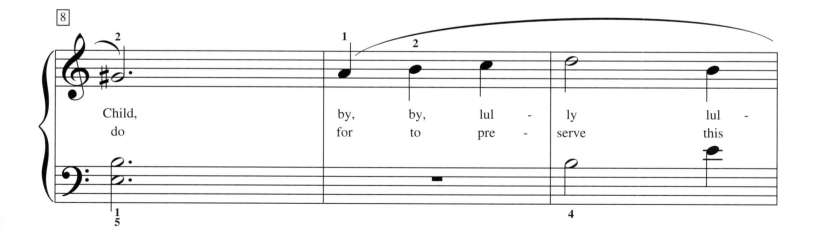

Child, by, by, lul - ly lul -
do for to pre - serve this

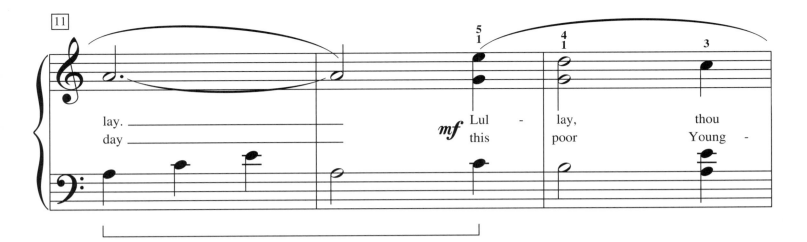

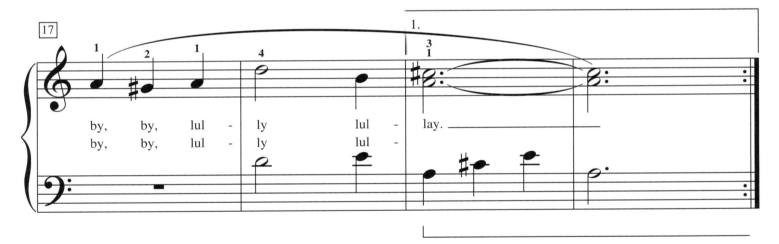

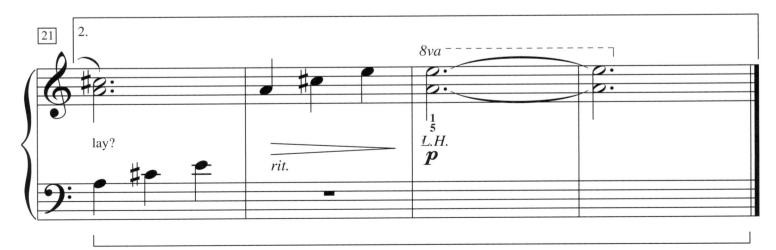

Pat-A-Pan

Secondo

Music by Bernard de la Monnoye
Arranged by Carol Klose

Medium March tempo (♩ = 104-120)

TRACKS 21/22

Both hands play one octave lower than written throughout.

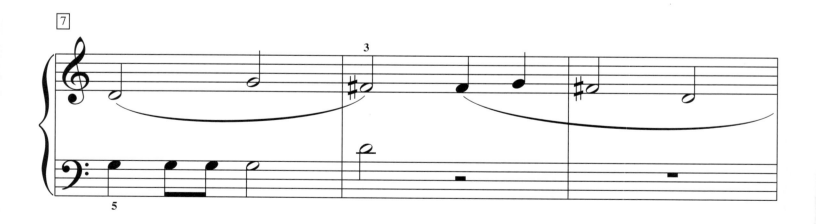

Pat-A-Pan

Primo

Music by Bernard de la Monnoye
Arranged by Carol Klose

Medium March tempo (♩ = 104-120)   TRACKS 23/24

Both hands play one octave higher than written throughout.

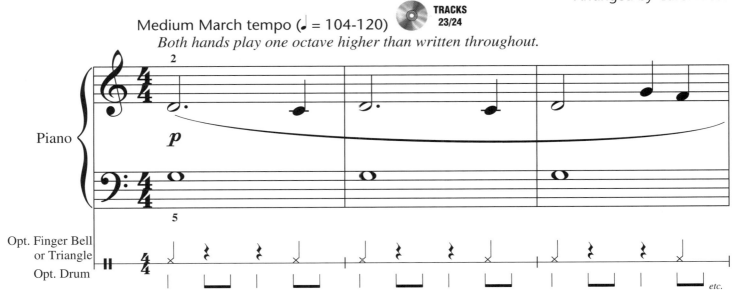

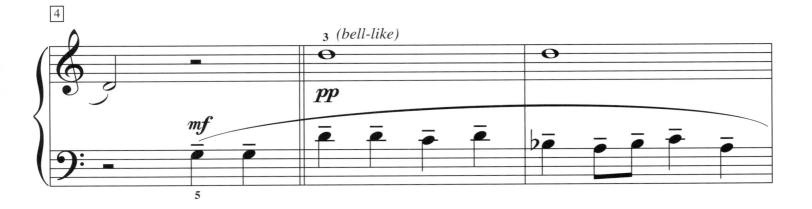

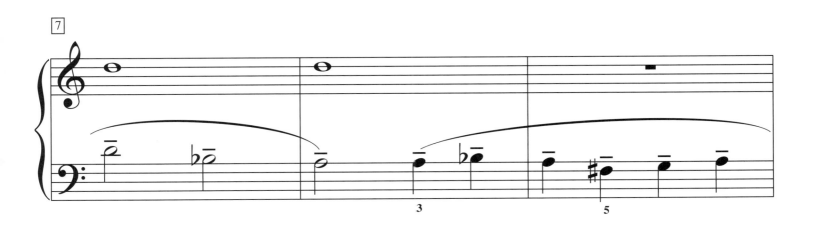

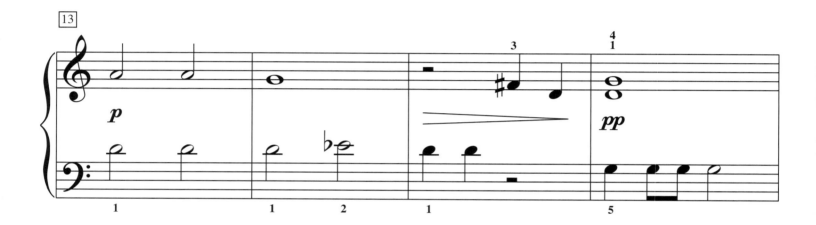

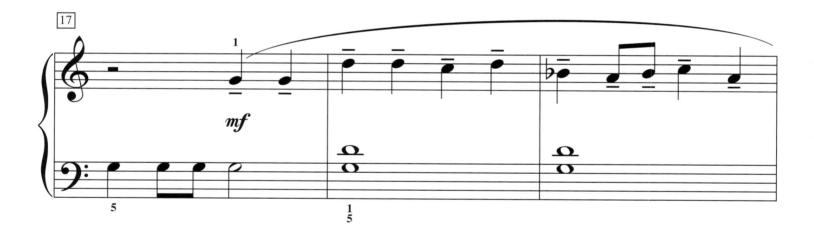

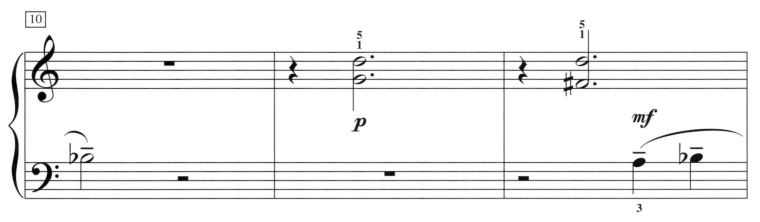

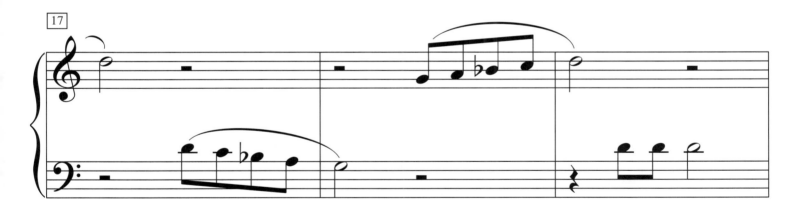

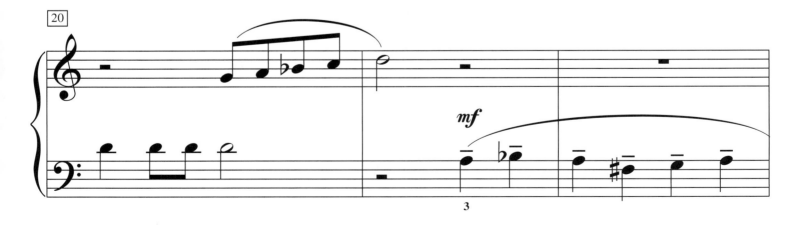

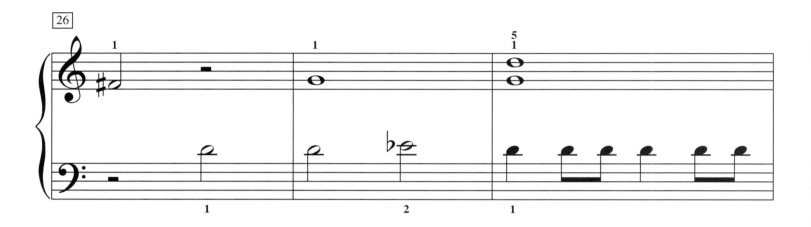

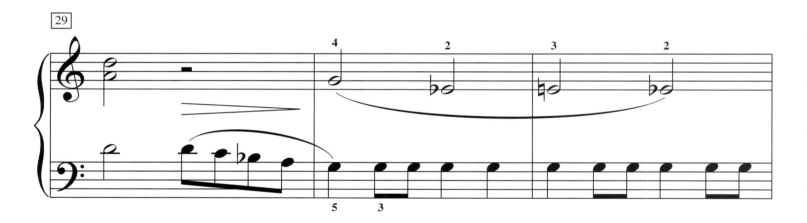

Opt. drum accompaniment ends here.

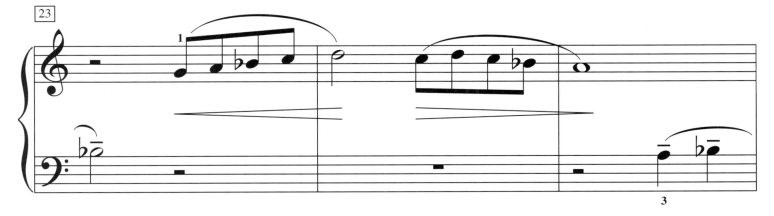

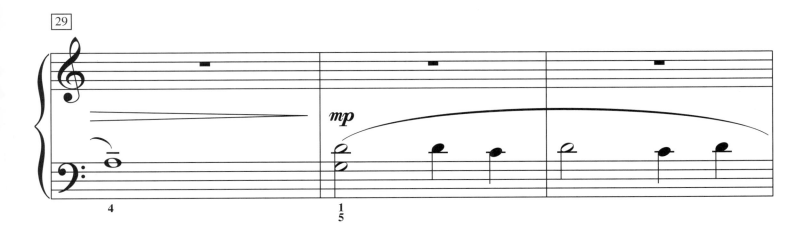

Opt. drum accompaniment ends here.

Silver and Gold

Music and Lyrics by
Johnny Marks
Arranged by Carol Klose

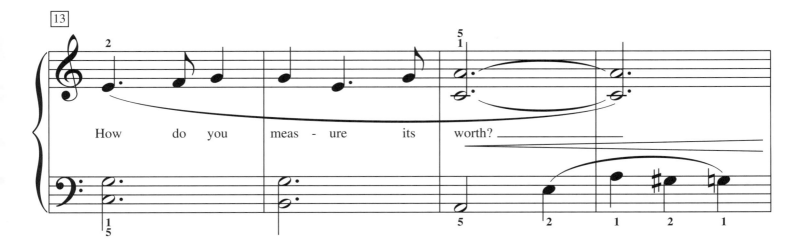

How do you meas - ure its worth? _____

Just by the pleas - ure it gives here on

mf

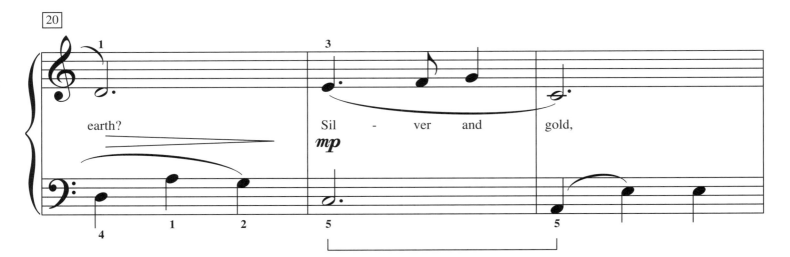

earth? Sil - ver and gold,

mp

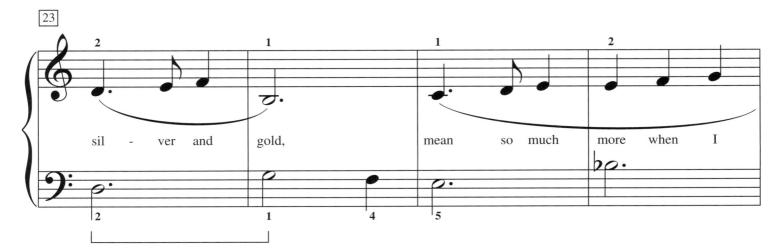

sil - ver and gold, mean so much more when I

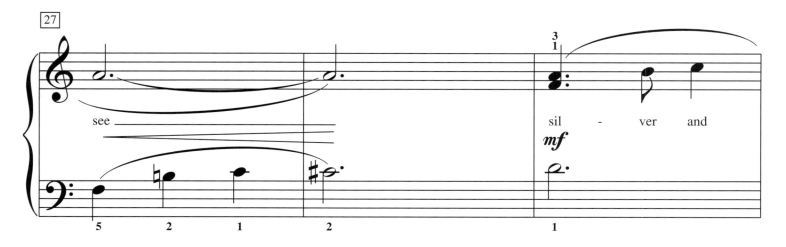

see _____ sil - ver and

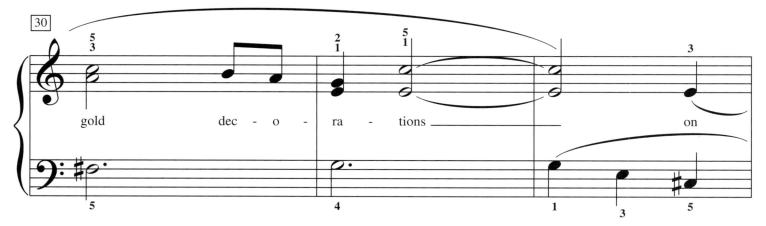

gold dec - o - ra - tions _____ on

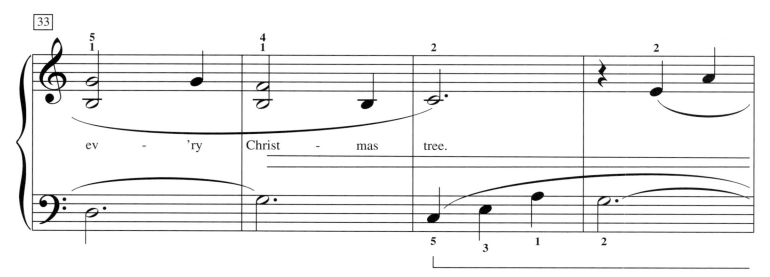

ev - 'ry Christ - mas tree.

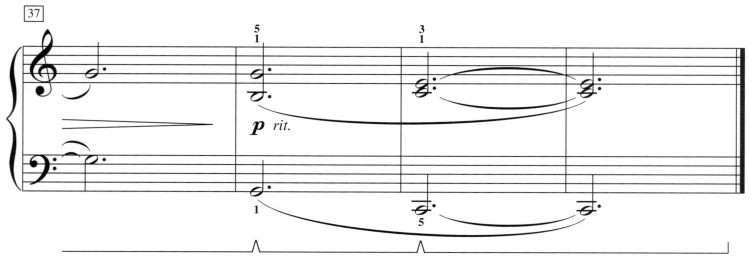

p rit.

This series showcases the varied talents of our **Hal Leonard Student Piano Library** family of composers.

Here is where you will find great original piano music by your favorite composers, including Phillip Keveren, Carol Klose, Jennifer Linn, Bill Boyd, and many others. Carefully graded for easy selection, each book contains gems that are certain to become tomorrow's classics!

EARLY ELEMENTARY

JAZZ PRELIMS
by Bill Boyd
HL00290032   12 Solos........................$5.95

ELEMENTARY

JAZZ STARTERS I
by Bill Boyd
HL00290425   10 Solos........................$6.95

JUST PINK
by Jennifer Linn
HL00296722   9 Solos.........................$5.95

MUSICAL MOODS
by Phillip Keveren
HL00296714   7 Solos.........................$5.95

PUPPY DOG TALES
by Deborah Brady
HL00296718   5 Solos.........................$6.95

LATE ELEMENTARY

CIRCUS SUITE
by Mona Rejino
HL00296665   5 Solos.........................$5.95

CORAL REEF SUITE
by Carol Klose
HL00296354   7 Solos.........................$5.95

IMAGINATIONS IN STYLE
by Bruce Berr
HL00290359   7 Solos.........................$5.95

JAZZ STARTERS II
by Bill Boyd
HL00290434   11 Solos........................$6.95

JAZZ STARTERS III
by Bill Boyd
HL00290465   12 Solos........................$6.95

LES PETITES IMAGES
by Jennifer Linn
HL00296664   7 Solos.........................$6.95

MOUSE ON A MIRROR
by Phillip Keveren
HL00296361   5 Solos.........................$6.95

PLAY THE BLUES!
by Luann Carman (Method Book)
HL00296357   10 Solos........................$8.99

SHIFTY-EYED BLUES
by Phillip Keveren
HL00296374   5 Solos.........................$6.95

TEX-MEX REX
by Phillip Keveren
HL00296353   6 Solos.........................$5.95

THROUGHOUT THE YEAR
by Christos Tsitsaros
HL00296723   12 Duets.......................$6.95

THE TOYMAKER'S WORKSHOP
by Deborah Brady
HL00296513   5 Duets........................$5.95

TRADITIONAL CAROLS FOR TWO
arr. by Carol Klose
HL00296557   5 Duets........................$7.99

EARLY INTERMEDIATE

DANCES FROM AROUND THE WORLD
by Christos Tsitsaros
HL00296688   7 Solos.........................$6.95

FANCIFUL WALTZES
by Carol Klose
HL00296473   5 Solos.........................$7.95

JAZZ BITS AND PIECES
by Bill Boyd
HL00290312   11 Solos........................$6.95

MONDAY'S CHILD
by Deborah Brady
HL00296373   7 Solos.........................$6.95

PORTRAITS IN STYLE
by Mona Rejino
HL00296507   6 Solos.........................$6.95

THINK JAZZ!
by Bill Boyd (Method Book)
HL00290417..................................$9.95

THE TWELVE DAYS OF CHRISTMAS
arr. Deborah Brady
HL00296531   13 Solos........................$6.95

WORLD GEMS
arr. Amy O'Grady (Piano Ens./2 Pianos, 8 Hands)
HL00296505   6 Folk Songs $6.95

INTERMEDIATE

AMERICAN IMPRESSIONS
by Jennifer Linn
HL00296471   6 Solos $7.95

ANIMAL TONE POEMS
by Michele Evans
HL00296439   10 Solos........................$6.95

CHRISTMAS IMPRESSIONS
by Jennifer Linn
HL00296706   8 Solos.........................$6.95

CONCERTO FOR YOUNG PIANISTS
by Matthew Edwards (2 Pianos, 4 Hands)
HL00296356   Book/CD....................$16.95

CONCERTO NO. 2 IN G MAJOR
by Matthew Edwards (2 Pianos, 4 Hands)
HL00296670   3 Movements.............$16.95

DAKOTA DAYS
by Sondra Clark
HL00296521   5 Solos.........................$6.95

DESERT SUITE
by Carol Klose
HL00296667   6 Solos.........................$6.95

7777 W. BLUEMOUND RD. P.O. BOX 13819 MILWAUKEE, WI 53213

FAVORITE CAROLS FOR TWO
arr. Sondra Clark
HL00296530   5 Duets........................$6.95

FLORIDA FANTASY SUITE
by Sondra Clark
HL00296766   3 Duets........................$7.95

ISLAND DELIGHTS
by Sondra Clark
HL00296666   4 Solos.........................$6.95

JAMBALAYA
by Eugénie Rocherolle (2 Pianos, 8 Hands)
HL00296654   Piano Ensemble............$9.95

JAZZ DELIGHTS
by Bill Boyd
HL00240435   11 Solos........................$6.95

JAZZ FEST
by Bill Boyd
HL00240436   10 Solos........................$6.95

JAZZ MOODS
by Tony Caramia
HL00296728   8 Solos.........................$6.95

JAZZ SKETCHES
by Bill Boyd
HL00220001   8 Solos.........................$6.95

LES PETITES IMPRESSIONS
by Jennifer Linn
HL00296355   6 Solos.........................$6.95

MELODY TIMES TWO
arr. by Eugénie Rocherolle
HL00296360   4 Duets.......................$12.95

**MONDAY'S CHILD
(A CHILD'S BLESSINGS)**
by Deborah Brady
HL00296373   7 Solos.........................$6.95

POETIC MOMENTS
by Christos Tsitsaros
HL00296403   8 Solos.........................$7.95

ROMP!
by Phillip Keveren
(Digital Ensemble/6 Keyboards, 6 Players)
HL00296549   Book/CD....................$9.95
HL00296548   Book/GM Disk $9.95

SONATINA HUMORESQUE
by Christos Tsitsaros
HL00296772   3 Movements...............$6.99

SONGS WITHOUT WORDS
by Christos Tsitsaros
HL00296506   9 Solos.........................$7.95

SUITE DREAMS
by Tony Caramia
HL00296775   4 Solos.........................$6.99

TALES OF MYSTERY
by Jennifer Linn
HL00296769   6 Solos.........................$7.99

THREE ODD METERS
by Sondra Clark (1 Piano, 4 Hands)
HL00296472   3 Duets $6.95

0109